Wandering and Thinking and Hiking

But Not Necessarily in that Order

LuAnne Nickell Prevost

Wandering and Thinking and Hiking
ISBN: Softcover 978-1-960326-02-7
Copyright 2022 by LuAnne Nickell Prevost

All rights reserved. No part of this book may be reproduced or transmitted in any form or by any means, electronic or mechanical, including photocopying, recording, or by any information storage and retrieval system, without permission in writing from the publisher.

Parson's Porch Books is an imprint of Parson's Porch & Company (PP&C) in Cleveland, Tennessee. PP&C is a self-funded charity which earns money by publishing books of noted authors, representing all genres. Its face and voice is **David Russell Tullock** (dtullock@parsonsporch.com).

Parson's Porch & Company turns books into bread & milk by sharing its profits with the poor.

www.parsonsporch.com

Wandering and Thinking and Hiking

But Not Necessarily in that Order

Dedication

To my beloved children; Gabriella, Phillip and Lydia. May you always experience an abundance of unconditional love.

The fairest thing in nature, a flower, still has its roots in earth and manure.

-**D. H. Lawrence**, English writer, novelist, poet, essayist (1885-1930)

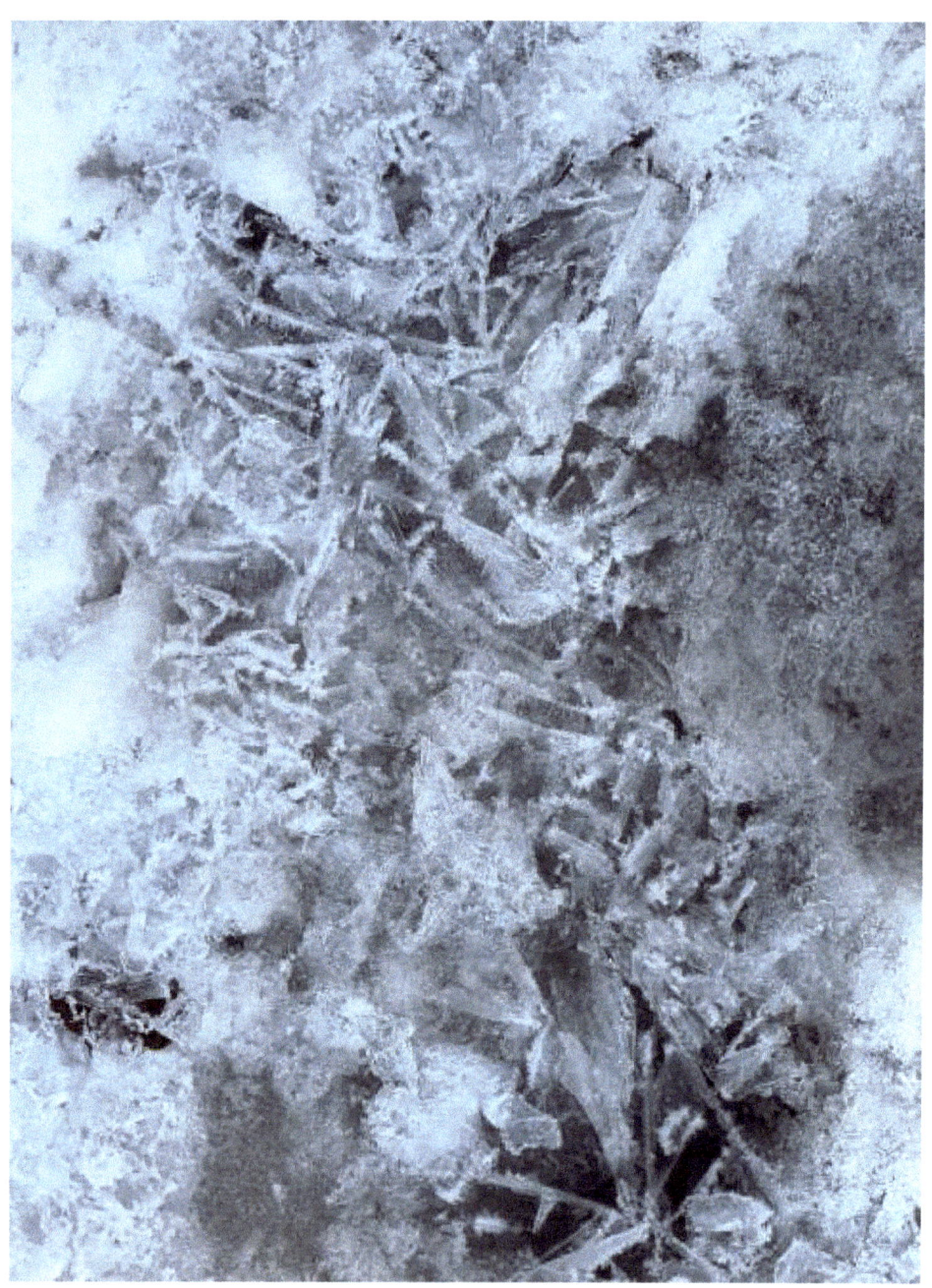

May I have the courage today
To live the life that I would love,
To postpone my dream no longer
But do at last what I came here for
And waste my heart on fear no more.

-John O'Donohue, Irish poet, author, priest, philosopher, (1956-2008)

Foreword

The summer of 2019 began a journey of curiosity, grief, persistence and in all honesty, fear. On February 26, 2014, two loving and distinguished gentlemen left this earth; my father, Rev. Joseph Nickell and my former father-in-law, Dr. Gibbs Prevost. The loss of these two, and on the same day, began my travels of self-discovery, intrigue, and a deeper sense of loss and hope.

Not only did my father die, but my mother suffered a stroke which resulted in greater memory loss and a reliance on caretakers. At my father's funeral, delayed a month due to my mother's requirement to complete physical rehabilitation services, Carolyn Blevins responded with these words, "You've had a hell of a ride." She was not wrong. My mother continued to decline and on July 25, 2019, she died after residing in a memory care unit for only two months.

Watching Mary Nickell, a determined, hospitable and stubborn woman, decline for four years could be described as a revelatory moment. I inherited my mother's determination and independent spirit, and that spirit was telling me to move onward. I sold my house, put everything in storage, quit my job, but NOT my profession, and decided to work in national parks; Yellowstone and the Grand Tetons so far.

As the events of 2020's covid pandemic loomed large the level of suffering was not lost on me. My isolation took place in the frozen tundra of the Grand Tetons, and worried for my family, as we were 2000 miles apart. Winter thawed the earth but covid was alive and well, and unfortunately thriving and spreading. Isolation continued, resulting in loss of lives, confusion, inability to have personal interactions, cancellation of sentinel events, mental and physical fatigue.

Being a part of nature was my way to cope with the isolation and sadness surrounding my spirit. The pictures I had taken were ways to save those uplifting moments and thought the beauty might be helpful for others. Facebook and Instagram were my medium for sharing and the responses were overwhelming. Social media influence was not my goal. Sending pictures that might elicit peace, comfort and solace was my purpose.

Two people dear to my heart and soul, Rev. Mary Beth Duke and Rev. Sharon Youngs, asked when my pictures would be published in a meditation book. Their urgings, David Tullock and Parson's Porch are the catalyst for these meditations.

My travels have been varied; alone, accompanied by family and friends or with travelers along the way. I am grateful for good health, and for now good knees. The opportunity in front of me is not taken for granted.

Shalom.

> When you have worn out your shoes,
> the strength of the shoe leather has passed
> into the fiber of your body...
> [she] is the richest [woman] who
> pays the largest debt to [her] shoemaker.
>
> —Emerson

In nature, nothing is perfect, and everything is perfect. Trees can be contorted, bent in weird ways, and they're still beautiful.

-**Alice Walker**, American novelist, short story writer, poet, social activist, 1st African American woman to win the Pulitzer Prize for Fiction for the novel, *The Color Purple*, b. 1944

I believe the world is incomprehensibly beautiful - an endless prospect of magic and wonder.

-Ansel Adams, American landscape photographer and environmentalist (1902-1984)

The Great Spirit is in all things. He is in the air we breathe. The Great Spirit is our Father, but the Earth is our Mother. She nourishes us ... That which we put into the ground she returns to us.

―Big Thunder Wabanaki, Algonquin

What is Life? It is the flash of a firefly in the night. It is the breath of a buffalo in the wintertime. It is the little shadow which runs across the grass and loses itself in the sunset.

The True Peace. The first peace, which is the most important, is that which comes within the souls of people when they realize their relationship, their oneness, with the universe and all its powers, and when they realize where the center of the universe dwells Wakan-Taka (the Great Spirit), and that this center is really everywhere, it is within each of us. This is the real peace, and the others are but reflections of this. The second peace is that which is made between two individuals, and the third is that which is made between two nations. But above all you should understand that there can never be peace between nations until there is known that true peace, which, as I have often said, is within the souls of men.

-Black Elk, Oglala Sioux and Spiritual Leader, 2nd cousin of Crazy Horse, fought in the Battle of Little Bighorn, survived the Wounded Knee Massacre (1863-1950)

You have noticed that everything an Indian does in a circle, and that is because the Power of the World always works in circles, and everything and everything tries to be round.

In the old days all our power came to us from the sacred hoop of the nation and so long as the hoop was unbroken the people flourish. The flowering tree was the living center of the hoop, and the circle of the four quarters nourished it. The east gave peace and light, the south gave warmth, the west gave rain and the north with its cold and mighty wind gave strength and endurance.

This knowledge came to use from the outer world with our religion. Everything the power of the world does is done in a circle.

The sky is round, and I have heard that the earth is round like a ball and so are all the stars. The wind, in its greatest power, whirls.

Birds make their next in circles, for theirs is the same religion as ours.

The sun comes forth and goes down again in a circle. The moon does the same and both are round. Even the seasons form a great circle in their changing and always come back again to where they were.

The life of a man is a circle from childhood to childhood, and so it is in everything where power moves. Our teepees were round like the nests of birds, and these were always set in a circle, the nation's hoop, a nest of many nests, where the Great Spirit meant for us to hatch our children.

Black Elk, Holy Man of the Oglala Sioux (1863-1950)

Over a hundred years ago Black Elk has a vision of the time when Indian people would heal from the devastating effects of European migration. In his vision the Sacred Hoop which had been broken, would be mended in seven generations.

The children born into this decade will be the seventh generation.

Bless This House

This song is in the music app on my phone, and when I need a source of comfort, I listen to this song. It is a very special song as my father sang it often. He had a beautiful bass voice, with little or no formal training. When he officiated weddings, he oftentimes was the vocalist for the wedding as well. The Minister of Music at our church, Faye Brandon, had a gorgeous soprano voice, and they sang duets on a regular basis. Usually, the accompanist for my father was Martha Nevils, a very gifted organist and pianist. She was ever the attentive accompanist as Daddy took liberties with the tempo and note lengths, and Mrs. Nevils always adjusted to stay with him.

At my father's funeral, my family chose to end the service with a recording of him singing, *Bless This House*. Several years earlier he recorded various pieces, and it seemed fitting that the final words of his funeral would be a blessing from him, as he had blessed us so many times.

Bless this house, O Lord we pray,
Make it safe by night and day.
Bless these walls so firm and stout,
Keeping want and trouble out.

Bless the roof and chimneys tall,
Let thy peace lie overall.
Bless this door that it may prove,
Ever open to joy and love.

Bless these windows shining bright,
Letting in God's heavenly light.
Bless the hearth a blazing there,
With smoke ascending like a prayer.

Bless the people here within,
Keep them pure and free from sin.
Bless us all that we may be,
Fit O lord to dwell with Thee.

Bless us all that one day we
May dwell O Lord with Thee.

-Lyrics, Mahalia Jackson

Bob Gunton

In 1963, the Paul and Mary Crabtree Family moved to Crossville, Tennessee with a plan to make our small town a mecca of music, art, and theatre. The Cumberland County Playhouse, which continues to this day, opened in the summer of 1965 with *Tennessee, USA!* Written by Paul Crabtree, it is a musical celebration of Tennessee's history. The actors, singers, dancers, musicians, and wardrobe seamstresses were Crossville's school children, lawyers, insurance agents, schoolteachers, ministers, stay-at-home mother's; essentially, the members of the community.

There was one particular character who needed to be "a talented guy who played the guitar and sang pretty well." He was discovered by James (Jim Bob) Crabtree, the eldest son, who was a student at the Paulist Seminary St. Peter's College in Baltimore. Jim Bob's friend, Bob Gunton, was a fellow seminarian who also was studying for the priesthood.

Yes, THAT Bob Gunton, more affectionately referred to as Warden Norton in *The Shawshank Redemption*. "I believe in two things: Discipline and *The Bible*. Here you'll receive both. Put your trust in the Lord. Your ass belongs to me. Welcome to Shawshank."

Bob played the role of Johnny Timberlake, a strong, handsome man who played the guitar and sang pretty well and took on the role of the "good guy" who tried to influence historical decisions. He played this role from 1965-1968. He was replaced in 1969 because Vietnam called, and he served until 1971, and was a Bronze Star recipient.

As you can see, Bob did not become a priest, but his acting career took off. His role of Juan Peron in *Evita* and Sweeney Todd in *Sweeney Todd: The Demon Barber of Fleet Street* (1989 revival) brought him Tony Award nominations. He has performed on Broadway, television, and film, often portrayed as the strict, authoritarian character. Just Google him; I believe you will recognize him immediately.

In the summer of 2012, Bob, accompanied by his lovely wife, Carey, returned to the Cumberland County Playhouse to perform and star in his script, *Walking on Water*, a musical journey of theatre and song. My mother, father, and I attended the performance and enjoyed it very much. Afterwards, we lingered, hoping to speak with Bob, as we didn't know if he would be available. As he was greeting guests, my mother introduced herself and my father. Bob's face lit with recognition and exclaimed, "Preacher Nickell," and he embraced my father with the biggest bear hug I have ever witnessed. In 1965, my father sang in the chorus of *Tennessee, USA!* Bob remembered my father, his beautiful bass voice, and that he was a minister. This embrace of my father was Bob's most memorable performance, as he gave dignity, recognition, respect and genuine love to my father, whose body and brain were riddled with Alzheimer's disease. Bob humanized my father, and I will be forever grateful that he chose to exhibit gentleness, compassion, and genuine care. A few years before my father died, we were listening to music from *Tennessee, USA!*, and when I asked Daddy if he remembered Bob's voice, he responded, "Yes, I remember him. He was a man of good character."

When my parents died, Bob sent beautiful words of condolences and exhibited true kindness. He is a well-known and talented actor, and the words of Micah 6:8 seem to be a good example of Bob's life. "Humans, you have already been told what is good, what God wants of you-be fair to others, love kindness and loyalty and walk humbly with your God." On that day, Bob was the embodiment of Micah 6:8. Joseph and Mary Nickell talked about that day for months on end.

Brothers

When your bedroom is next to your brother's bedroom, even with the doors closed, there is much one can learn in life (I know what you are thinking!) What I learned from my brothers was good music. At an early age, I had a large repertoire of popular musical knowledge. Even though I didn't own the album, I knew every word of Elton John's *Yellow Brick Road*, except for *Rocketman*, which still confuses me. Chicago, with the amazing brass section, was listened to often, as Tim played the trumpet, trombone, tuba and sousaphone in the high school band. *Jeremiah Was A Bullfrog*, by Three Dog Night, was my favorite, along with Bread, The Doobie Brothers, America with *The Horse With No Name*, Crosby, Stills, Nash and Young, and even The Lettermen.

Not only did I have musical influence from my brothers, but I also received knowledge in sports, especially football. I was the only young girl on my street, as it was full of boys, and if I wanted to have fun, I played touch football in the front yard. My knowledge increased as I watched Mark play football for our high school team, and I was the most vocal, and perhaps most annoying fan cheering for #83.

New Year's Day was a big deal in our home, as it was college football bowl gameday. We unfolded the pull-out sofa, filled it with fluffy pillows, popped popcorn, drank lots of Dr. Pepper, and watched every single bowl game that was played. At some point in time we had two televisions, and were able to watch ABC, CBS and NBC. Daddy, Tim and Mark loved college football and I learned a great deal about holding, touchdowns, safety, going for 2, offsides, encroachment, illegal use of hands, face mask, flea flicker, Statue of Liberty play, "I" formation, shotgun, blitz, naked bootleg, sweep, and option play. My enjoyment of college football continues today, as I wear the colors of The Big Orange, and can sing every verse of *Rocky Top*.

When they were kids, I thought my brothers were going to kill each other, but they did grow out of that time period. I am grateful to have two brothers who are strong men of character, who are loyal to their family, and care for the well-being of others.

If you wish to know the divine, feel the wind on your face and the warm sun on your hand.

-**Buddha**, ascetic and spiritual teacher, founder of Buddhism, lived during 6th or 5th century BCE

Preserve and cherish the pale blue dot, it's the only home we've ever known.

-**Carl Sagan**, American astronomer, planetary scientist, cosmologist, astrophysicist, astrobiologist, author, science communicator (1934-1996)

Cherokee Prayer Blessing

May the Warm Winds of Heaven
Blow softly upon your house.
May the Great Spirit
Bless all who enter there.
May your Moccasins
Make happy tracks
in many snows,
and may the Rainbow
Always touch your shoulder.

May the stars carry your sadness away.
May the flowers fill your heart with beauty.
May hope forever to wipe away your tears.
And above all, may silence make you strong.

-Chief Dan George, Tsleil-Waututh Nation, actor, musician, poet, author (1899-1981)

We must protect the forests for our children, grandchildren and children yet to be born. We must protect the forests for those who can't speak for themselves such as the bird, animals, fish and trees.

-**Qwatsinas** (Hereditary Chief Edward Moody), Nuxalk Nation, visionary who strove for justice and protection of nature

If the white man wants to live in peace with the
Indian, he can live in peace...
Treat all men alike. Give them all the
same law. Give them all an even change
to live and grow. All men were made by
the same Great Spirit Chief.
They are all brothers. The Earth is the mother of
all people, and all people should have
equal rights upon it...
Let me be a free man, free to travel,
free to stop, free to work, free to trade
where I choose my own teachers,
free to follow the religion of my fathers,
free to think and talk and act for myself,
and I will obey every law or submit to the penalty.

-Heinmot Tooyalaket (Chief Joseph), Nez Perce Leader

There is a road in the hearts of all of us, hidden and seldom traveled, which leads to an unknown, secret place.

The old people came literally to love the soil, and they sat or reclined on the ground with a feeling of being close to a mothering power.

Their teepees were built upon the earth and their altars were made of earth.

The soul was soothing, strengthening, cleaning and healing.

That is why the old Indian still sits upon the earth instead of propping himself up and away from its life-giving forces.

For him, to sit or lie upon the ground is to be able to think more deeply and to feel more keenly. He can see more clearly into the mysteries of life and come closer in kinship to other lives about him.

Chief Luther Standing Bear Sicangu and Oglala Lakota author, educator, philosopher and actor. Worked to preserve Lakota culture and sovereignty, was at the forefront of a Progressive movement to change government policy toward Native Americans. (1868-1939)

I have heard you intend to settle us on a reservation near the mountains. I don't want to settle. I love to roam over the prairies. There I feel free and happy, but when we settle down we grow pale and die.

-**Chief Satanta**, Kiowa war chief and orator (ca 1820-1878)

Humankind has not woven the web of life. We are but one thread within it. Whatever we do to the web, we do to ourselves. All things are bound together. All things connect.

-Chief Seattle, Suquamish and Duwamish chief, pursued a path of accommodation to white settlers, Seattle, Washington named for him (1790-1866)

So live your life that the fear of death can never enter your heart.

Trouble no one about their religion; respect others in their view, and demand that they respect yours.

Love your life, perfect your life, beautify all things in your life.

See to make your life long and its purpose in the service of your people.

Prepare a noble death song for the day when you go over the great divide.

Always give a word or a sign of salute when meeting or passing a friend, even a stranger, when in a lonely place.

Show respect to all people and grovel to none.

When you arise in the morning give thanks for the food and for the joy of living.

If you see no reason for giving thanks, the fault lies only in yourself.

Abuse no one and no thing, for abuse turns the wise ones to fools And robs the spirit of its vision.

When it comes your time to die, be not like those whose hearts are filled with the fear of death, so that when their time comes they weep and pray for a little more time to live their lives over again in a different way.

Sing your death song and die like a hero going home.

-**Chief Tecumseh** (Crouching Tiger) Shawnee Nation (1768-1813)

Climbing Song

Away, away, - to the mountains away,
Where the pine trees murmur and sway,
And the foamy waterfalls sing and spring
Over the boulders gray.

The hidden beauties will lure you on,
'Till your heart from its dreaming is drawn,
And your eyes are bright with the free delight
Known to the fearless fawn.

Fear not to weary - you never can tire,
For the sunshine gives you its fire,
And your feet will follow the breeze with ease,
Higher and ever higher.

-Ruby Archer, American poet (1873-1961)

Columbines

Airily poised in the garden bed,
Delicate saffron, white and rose,
With gossamer petals lightly spread
The columbines flutter upon their toes.

Wait, till the moonlight sets them free!
They'll stir, they'll shake off the dew, they'll go
Dancing, dancing (but you'll not see–
You'll be too busy asleep to know.)

Someone surprised them once in May,
Glimmering ivory, gold and pink,
Dancing under the moon. That way
Columbine found their name, I think.

-**Teresa Hooley**, English poet (1888-1973)

Hold on to what is good,
Even if it's a handful of earth.

Hold on to what you believe,
Even if it's a tree that stands by itself.

Hold on to what you must do,
Even if it's a long way from here.

Hold on to your life,
Even if it's easier to let go.

Hold on to my hand,
Even if someday I'll be gone away from you.

-**Crowfoot**, Blackfoot warrior and orator (1830-1890)

Just one small positive thought in the morning can change your whole day.

-**Dalai Lama XIV**, highest spiritual leader and former head of state of Tibet, b. 1935

If you have not touched the rocky wall of a canyon.

If you have not heard a rushing river pound over cobblestones.

If you have not seen a native trout rise in a crystalline pool beneath a shattering riffle, or a golden eagle spread its wings and cover you in shadow.

If you have not seen the tree line recede to the top of a bare crested mountain.

If you have not looked into a pair of wild eyes and seen your own reflection.

Please, for the good of your soul, travel west.

-Daniel J. Rice, *This Side of a Wilderness*, b.1979

I just wish the world was twice as big and half of it was still unexplored.

-David Attenborough, English biologist, broadcaster, natural historian, author, b. 1926

Light of a Clear Blue Morning

It's been a long dark night
And I've been a waitin' for the morning
It's been a long hard fight
But I see a brand-new day a dawning
I've been looking for the sunshine
You know I ain't seen it in so long
But everything's gonna work out just fine
And everything's gonna be all right
That's been all wrong

'Cause I can see the light of a clear blue morning
I can see the light of a brand-new day
I can see the light of a clear blue morning
Oh, and everything's gonna be all right
It's gonna be okay

It's been a long, long time
Since I've known the taste of freedom
And those clinging vines
That had me bound, well I don't need 'em
Oh, I've been like a captured eagle, you know an eagle's born to fly
Now that I have won my freedom, like an eagle I am eager for the sky

And I can see the light of a clear blue morning
I can see the light of brand-new day
I can see the light of a clear blue morning
Oh, and everything's gonna be all right
It's gonna be okay

I can see the light of a clear blue morning
I can see the light of brand-new day
I can see the light of a clear blue morning
Ooh, everything's gonna be all right
Everything's gonna be all right
Everything's gonna be all right
It's gonna be okay

And I can see the light of a clear blue morning
I can see the light of a brand-new day
I can see the light of a clear blue morning
Ooh and everything's gonna be all right
Everything's gonna be all right
Everything's gonna be all right
It's gonna be okay

I can see the light of a clear blue morning
I can see the light of brand-new day
I can see the light of a clear blue morning
Everything's gonna be all right
Everything's gonna be all right
Everything's gonna be all right
It's gonna be okay

-**Dolly Parton**, singer, performer, philanthropist, song writer, businesswoman. This song was written in 1976, driving home from a contentious conversation with Porter Wagoner as she left his show and began her solo career. b. 1946

Earth, Teach Me

Earth teach me quiet ~
as the grasses are still with new light.

Earth teach me suffering ~
as old stones suffer with memory.

Earth teach me humility ~
as blossoms are humble with beginning.

Earth teach me caring ~
as mothers nurture their young.

Earth teach me courage ~
as the tree that stands alone.

Earth teach me limitation ~
as the ant that crawls on the ground.

Earth teach me freedom ~
as the eagle that soars in the sky.
Earth teach me acceptance ~
as the leaves that die each fall.

Earth teach me renewal ~
as the seed that rises in the spring.

Earth teach me to forget myself ~
as melted snow forgets its life.

Earth teach me to remember kindness ~
as dry fields weep with rain.

~An Ute Prayer

To make a prairie it takes a clover and one bee,
One clover, and a bee,
And revery.
The revery alone will do,
If bees are few.

-**Emily Dickinson**, *American poet (1830-1886)*

Faye Brandon

There are significant people in our lives who shape and mold us into the adults we become. For me, that woman was Faye Brandon. Not only did she shape and mold me, but she impacted just about every child who walked into her choir room at First Baptist Church in Crossville, Tennessee. When our family moved to Crossville, in 1962, Faye was the Minister of Music at First Baptist Church where my father would serve as the pastor for 16 years. Faye was gifted with a beautiful soprano voice and shared her musicianship with the church and the community, including the 1965 opening of the Cumberland County Playhouse performance of *Tennessee, USA!*

Children's choir was serious business, and when we rehearsed, we always improved. Faye always praised us, but also expected us to take our knowledge for better vocal production. As we began to improve, we performed for adjudication by professional musicians at Tennessee Baptist choral events and always received superior ratings. By the time we were in junior high and high school, large musical productions were part of our lives, and they were fun. If you were raised in a Baptist church, you probably sang *Celebrate Life*. Our productions were carefully rehearsed and produced with great professionalism. At Faye's memorial service the following words were eloquently spoken by my brother,

Tim Nickell: "Unknown to any of us, we were living in one of the most teachable moments of life. Note by note and measure by measure, both the goodness of Faye Brandon and the power of music changed all of us and opened up a world to us that we didn't know existed. Faye was a difference-maker in our lives, and she gave us a gift that we could never repay. She left a remarkable, multi-dimensional, professional legacy."

Faye's memorial service was held in January 2022, with two of her children's choir members playing the organ and piano, and about a dozen singing in the choir. We are all grown up now but hold in our hearts Faye's influence, wisdom, and kindness.

"The Lord bless you and keep you. The Lord make Her face to shine upon you. And be gracious unto you. The Lord lift up Her countenance upon you and give you peace and give you peace."

チチ

Fog

The fog comes
on little cat feet.

It sits looking
over harbor and city
on silent haunches
and then moves on.

-Carl Sandburg, American poet, biographer, journalist, editor (1878-1967)

For the Chipmunk in My Yard

I think he knows I'm alive, having come down
The three steps of the back porch
And given me a good once over. All afternoon
He's been moving back and forth,
Gathering odd bits of walnut shells and twigs,
While all about him the great fields tumble
To the blades of the thresher. He's luck
To be where he is, wild with all that happens.
He's lucky he's not one of the shadows
Living in the blond heart of the wheat.
This autumn when trees bolt, dark with the fires
Of starlight, he'll curl among their roots,
Wanting nothing but the slow burn of matter
On which he fastens like a small, brown flame.

-Robert Gibb, American poet b. 1946

Lord, help us to maintain a reverent attitude toward nature, threatened from all sides today, in such a way that we may restore it completely to the condition of brother/sister and to its role of usefulness to all humankind for the glory of God the Creator.

-Franciscan prayer

I believe in God, only I spell it Nature.

-Frank Lloyd Wright, American architect, designer, writer, educator (1867-1959)

Lakota Instructions for Living

Friend do it this way - that is,
Whatever you do in life,
Do the very best you can
With both your heart and mind.

And if you do it that way,
The Power Of The Universe
Will come to your assistance,
If your heart and mind are in Unity.

When one sits in the Hoop Of The People,
One must be responsible because
All of Creation is related.
And the hurt of one is the hurt of all.
And the honor of one is the honor of all.
And whatever we do affects everything in the universe.

If you do it that way - that is,
If you truly join your heart and mind
As One - whatever you ask for,
That's the Way It's Going To Be.

Passed down from White Buffalo Calf Woman

Friends Since We Were Five

In 1965, we were introduced; I don't know the occasion, but it was the beginning of a deep friendship that continues today. Tammy Petty Brewer is my friend. We have shared so many life events, and at the rate we are going, we have many more to experience.

When we entered Mrs. McCuiston's first grade class, we were so excited to be in the same classroom. The following year we checked the classroom roster and discovered we were together in Mrs. Elmore's class. Third grade was probably our best year in Mrs. Irene Cooper's class, where she read aloud the entire Laura Ingalls Wilder series. We listened with great concentration as she read these books and transported us back to the days on the prairie. Fourth grade took place in Mrs. Brewer's class, and it was becoming evident that we were no longer going to be sitting together.

I have failed to mention that Tammy is petite, and as an adult, I have always known her as 4'11 ¾". On the other hand, I am 5'10", and we have been affectionately referred to as Mutt and Jeff. Our time together in Mrs. Brewer's class was spent on the playground since she sat in the front row of the class and I was further back, as I was getting taller by the day.

Fifth grade was when our idyllic life came to a screeching halt. We were not in the same classroom!!!!!!

It was awful, and then Tammy told me her family was moving to Middle Tennessee. She could have been moving to another country because my life was over. I don't remember very much about the physical move, but I did know my best friend was gone. No longer would we ride the go-cart Smokey in their backyard, still dressed in our Sunday's finest. No longer would we have science experiments in her secret closet. No longer would we trick or treat together. No more sleepovers or endless games of Go Fish or Yahtzee.

Little did we know our mothers were conspiring. Mary Nickell and Punky Petty knew how to keep us together. We wrote letters for years. I had boxes and boxes of letters from Tammy and am very sorry I did not keep them. Reading them today would be hilarious. My father's family lived in Middle Tennessee, and we frequently stopped at Tammy's house for a visit. At some point in time I remember Joe Petty asking Joe Nickell if it would be okay for me to stay at their house for the weekend. Oh gosh!! I was elated, a weekend with Tammy. Thankfully this turned into staying a week at Tammy's house, and then she would stay a week with me. When summer vacation arrived, I counted down the days to visit her house.

We are all grown up and have together traveled down some joyous paths and some difficult as well. Weddings, births of our children, loss of our parents, divorce, the death of her precious husband, and the beautiful wedding of her son.

Distance and time has not deterred our friendship. It seems we pick up exactly where we leave off. I have joked with Tammy that we need to choose our rocking chairs and pick out our retirement center so we can continue our claim, "We've been friends since we were five."

Go Forward With Courage

When you are in doubt, be still, and wait;
when doubt no longer exists for you,
then go forward with courage.
So long as mists envelop you, be still;
be still until the sunlight pours
through and dispels the mists
~ as it surely will.

Then act with courage.

Ponca Chief White Eagle (1800's to 1914)

Let us give thanks for the world around us.
Thanks for all the creatures, stones and plants.
Let us learn their lessons and seek their truths,
So that their path might be ours,
And we might live in harmony, a better life.

May the Earth continue to live,
May the heavens above continue to live,
May the rains continue to dampen the land,
May the wet forests continue to grow,
Then the flowers shall bloom
And we people shall live again.

-Hawaiian indigenous prayer

Through the silence of nature,
I attain Thy divine peace.
Oh sublime nature,
in thy stillness let my heart rest.
Thou are patiently awaiting the moment
to manifest through the silence of sublime nature.
Oh nature sublime, speak to me through silence,
for I am awaiting in silence like you the call of God.
Oh nature sublime,
through thy silence I hear Thy cry.
My heart is tuned to the quietness,
that the stillness of nature inspires.

-**Hazrat Inayat Khan**, Indian professor of musicology, singer, poet, philosopher (1882-1927)

Distance never separates two hearts that really care, for our memories span the miles and in seconds we are there. But whenever I start feeling sad cuz I miss you I remind myself how lucky I am to have someone so special to miss.

-**Henri J. M. Nouwen**, Dutch Catholic priest, professor, writer, theologian, left academia to work with individuals with intellectual and developmental disabilities at the L'Arche Daybreak Community (1932-1996)

I took a walk in the woods and came out taller than the trees.

-Henry David Thoreau, American naturalist, essayist, poet, philosopher (1817-1862)

God is the foundation for everything
This God undertakes, God gives.
Such that nothing that is necessary for life is lacking.

Now humankind needs a body that
at all times honors and praises God.
This body is supported in every way through earth.
Thus the earth glorifies the power of God.

-Hildegard of Bingen, German Benedictine abbess and polymath active as writer, composer, philosopher, mystic, visionary (1098-1179)

May the waters flow peacefully;
may the herbs and plants grow peacefully;
may all the divine powers bring unto us peace.
may the rain come down in the proper time,
may the earth yield plenty of corn,
may the country be free from war.
The supreme Lord is peace.

-Hindu prayer

Holy Envy

Barbara Brown Taylor, priest, scholar, theologian, preacher, author, and teacher, is one of my favorite women. She has been named one of the most influential people in the world, one of the twelve most effective preachers in the English-speaking world, and a top ten most influential living preacher. She has written 15 books, and I own 14 of them, several with her signature on the inside cover.

Her latest book I read was *Holy Envy: Finding God in the Faith of Others*. This book recounts the world religion class she taught at Piedmont College as she reflected on her spiritual journey and how it intersects with the religious traditions of others. "Part of my ongoing priesthood is to find the bridge between my faith and the faiths of other people, so that those of us who draw water from wells on different sides of the river can still get together from time to time, making the whole area safe for our children." (Taylor)

The words of her book were illuminating to me as I encountered a couple from Texas who were members of a spirit-filled church. (Their words, not mine.) I met this couple at a wedding in the Great Smoky Mountains National Park where I officiated. They were guests of the couple, and I sat with them at the reception. As we were talking, they asked me about my work outside of officiating weddings, and I explained I was a hospital chaplain. Their next question caught me completely off guard. "So when you visit patients, you see people who are not Christian? You visit with people who are Jewish and Catholic and people of other faiths?" I nodded yes. "Wow, that must be so hard when you know they are wrong." Well, you can imagine I was very surprised by their comment. I physically bit my tongue and explained that illness and death are not the times to evangelize but to offer comfort and support during a time of crisis. They nodded politely, and I honestly don't know what followed, as I was stunned. The next day I wished I was quick enough to have asked them a return question: What do you mean they are wrong? I wonder what kind of conversation would have ensued!

I have read *Holy Envy* twice and believe it is time for a third reading, as the idea of Christian Nationalism continues to thrive. When I hear the United States is a Christian nation, I wonder how different we would worship or look if the Europeans had chosen not to travel across the Atlantic but, instead, people from Asian countries were able to sail across the Pacific, or if Muslim nations had a fleet of ships that could traverse the seas. What if none of them arrived? We would be Native American and worship the beauty of Mother Earth. "Most of us like thinking we are God's only children….At least one of the purposes of church is to remind us that God has other children, easily as precious as we. Baptism and narcissism cancel each other out." (Taylor))

A friend once described God as a hike to Mount LeConte. There are about five trails that lead to the top; no matter which you choose, it gets you to the same place. Happy hiking!

Honor the sacred.
Honor the Earth, Our Mother.
Honor the Elders.
Honor all with whom we share the Earth.
Four-legged, two-legged, winged ones,
Swimmers, crawlers, plant and rock people.
Walk in balance and beauty.

-Native American Elder

In the Green Mountains

I dare not look away
From beauty such as this,

Lest, while my glance should stray,
Some loveliness I miss.

The trees might choose to print
Their shadow on the lake;

The windless air might glint
With aspen leaves that shake.

Over the mountains there
A thin blue veil might drift;

Then in a moment rare
This thin blue veil might lift.

Ah, I must pay good heed
To beauty such as this,

Lest, in some hour of need,
Its loveliness I miss.

-Jessie Belle Rittenhouse, Literary critic, poet (1869-1948)

One individual cannot possibly make a difference alone. It is individual efforts, collectively, that makes a noticeable difference - all the difference in the world!

-Dr. Jane Goodall, English primatologist and anthropologist, b. 1934

Listen to your life. See it for the fathomless mystery it is. In the boredom and pain of it, not less than in the excitement and gladness: touch, taste, smell your way to the holy and hidden heart of it, because in the last analysis all moments are key moments, and life itself is grace.

-**Frederick Buechner**, American writer, novelist, poet, autobiographer, essayist, preacher, theologian (1926-2022)

Before our white brothers arrived to make us civilized men, we didn't have any kind of prison. Because of this, we had no delinquents.

Without a prison, there can be no delinquents.

We had no locks nor keys and therefore among us there were no thieves.

When someone was so poor that he couldn't afford a horse, a tent or a blanket, he would, in that case, receive it all as a gift.

We were too uncivilized to give great importance to private property.

We didn't know any kind of money and consequently, the value of a human being was not determined by his wealth.

We had no written laws laid down, no lawyers, no politicians. Therefore we were not able to cheat and swindle one another.

We were really in bad shape before the white men arrived and I don't know how to explain how we were able to manage without these fundamental things that (so they tell us) are so necessary for a civilized society.

~John (Fire) Lame Deer, Sioux Lakota (1903-1976)

I go to nature to be soothed and healed, and to have my senses put in order.

-John Burroughs, American naturalist and nature essayist (1837-1921)

Going to the mountains is going home.

-**John Muir**, Scottish-American naturalist, author, early advocate for preservation of wilderness in the United States (1838-1914)

Sunshine is delicious, rain is refreshing
Wind braces us up, snow is exhilarating;
There is really no such thing as bad weather,
Only different kinds of good weather.

-**John Ruskin**, English writer, philosopher, art critic (1819-1900)

The goal of life is to make your heartbeat match the beat of the universe, to match your nature with Nature.

-Joseph Campbell, American writer (1904-1987)

Time spent amongst trees is never wasted time.

-Katrina Mayer, writer, motivational speaker, ordained interfaith minister, author of *The Mustard Seed*

Kay and Greg Reed

Sometimes there are people who enter your life, and you have no idea the impact they will have on you and your children. The two who have loved me and helped me parent my own children are Kay and Greg Reed. We first met at church in Knoxville, Tennessee, as Kay and Greg moved for employment at the University of Tennessee; Greg was in the engineering department and Kay was in the graduate school. We became friends, and at one time they were my Sunday School teachers, which offered more opportunities for a deeper friendship.

After my children were born, Kay and Greg took on a very important role in their development. Some of their best birthday parties were held at Kay and Greg's swimming pool, which included lots of decorations, as Kay was the consummate decorator. Greg was the steady and watchful lifeguard to make sure everyone was having fun, but also safe at the same time.

High tea was also a treat at the Reed household. Scones with lemon curd, cucumber sandwiches, petits-fours, and delicious cheese and crackers accompanied a variety of English tea, which was always served on beautiful fine China. We always dressed for the occasion and wore fancy hats to celebrate, and of course we always drank our tea with pinkies out.

Kay is an excellent cook and showed great patience as she included my children in the baking process. Cookies were one of our favorites; she was always finding new recipes to try, and, of course, we were happy to sample them. My son, Phillip, was especially influenced by Kay, as he graduated culinary school and is presently working in the restaurant industry with a goal of becoming an executive chef.

My oldest child, Lydia, was taken to Dollywood for the first time by Kay and Greg. They took her to football games, Lady Vol basketball games, and attended every dance and piano recital. When Phillip and Gabriella Kathleen (Kay's middle name) were born, Kay and Greg's involvement continued to grow, and they were indeed members of the family. My gratitude for their influence in the lives of my children can never be fully recognized, but when I find pictures of past birthday parties, visits to Dollywood, Easter egg hunts, Halloween parties, and high tea, I am reminded of their dedication and commitment to my children.

Our culture gives us guidelines for raising our children through books, magazines, podcasts, and television. Various African societies use proverbs to direct childhood:

In Lunyoro - "A child does not grow up only in a single home."

In Kihaya - "A child belongs not to one parent or home."

In Swahili - "Whomsoever is not taught by the mother will be taught with the world."

In Kijita - "Regardless of a child's biological parents, its upbringing belongs to the community."

Indeed, it does take a village to raise a child; I am grateful Kay and Greg Reed were willing to take on that task.

The environment, after all, is where we all meet, where we all have a mutual interest. It is one thing that all of us share. It is not only a mirror of ourselves, but a focusing lens on what we can become.

-Lady Bird Johnson, First Lady of the United States of America (1963-1969), Advocate for beautifying the nation's cities and highways, recipient of Presidential Medal of Freedom and Congressional Gold Medal, (1912-2007)

Lakota Prayer

Wakan Tanka, Great Mystery,
teach me how to trust
my heart,
my mind,
my intuition,
my inner knowing,
the senses of my body,
the blessings of my spirit.
Teach me to trust these things
so that I may enter my Sacred Space
and love beyond my fear,
and thus Walk in Balance
with the passing of each glorious Sun.

According to the Native People, the Sacred Space
is the space between exhalation and inhalation.
The Walk in Balance is to have Heaven (spirituality)
and Earth (physicality) in Harmony.

Nature does not hurry, yet everything is accomplished.

-**Lao Tzu**, ancient Chinese philosopher and writer, lived during 4th century, BCE

If you truly love nature, you will find beauty everywhere.

-Laura Ingalls Wilder, American writer, known for the *Little House on the Prairie* series, based on her childhood in a settler and pioneer family (1867-1957)

Listening

During my second year of seminary, my professor, Dr. Ircel Harrison, chose a textbook, *Holy Listening: The Art of Spiritual Direction*, by Rev. Margaret Guenther, (1930-2016), Professor Emerita of Ascetical Theology at The General Theological Seminary, where she served for many years as the Director of the Center for Christian Spirituality. I read this book, and immediately read it again. The subject of her book was exactly what I needed to read, as I was intent on becoming a hospital chaplain.

Listening is not a task in which society seems to excel. For years we have had talk radio channels and lots of "talking heads" on television. Stephen Covey says, "Most people don't listen with the intent to understand, they listen with the intent to reply." Let that quote sink in for a moment.

As a child in elementary school my teachers would often tell the class, "You have two ears and one mouth." They weren't wrong. We learn so much more when we listen more and talk less. In Lin Manuel-Miranda's, *Hamilton*, Aaron Burr tells Alexander Hamilton to "talk less, smile more." I believe talking less, and listening more is the key to better communication, understanding, and creating an atmosphere of trust.

All of us are living human documents. We have a story and many times; we just want someone to listen to what we have to say. Rev. Guenther said in her book, "Dear God, help me pay attention! Dear God, help me keep my mouth shut! Dear God, let me put myself out of the way!

Dear God, let me be wholly present to this person, your child!" As I sat at the bedside of patients, and families, I prayed these words, or a version of the prayer. When individuals are in pain, there are no words I can offer to take away their pain or fix the situation. Being present with open ears, and an open heart is all I can offer. Oftentimes, that's all that is needed.

Photograph captured by Gabriella Prevost

Nature has been for me, for as long as I remember, a source of solace, inspiration, adventure, and delight; a home, a teacher, a companion.

-Lorraine Anderson, freelance writer, editor and teacher whose work focuses on encouraging a way of life in tune with nature, b. 1952

To forget how to dig the earth and to tend the soil is to forget ourselves.

-**Mahatma Gandhi**, anti-colonial nationalist, political ethicist, employed nonviolent resistance to lead successful campaign for India's independence from British rule (1869-1945)

Mary Nickell

She was known by many names: Mary, Mary Ruth, Sis, Mrs. Nickell, Momma Nick, Nickie, and Momma. My mother was born in 1931 in Lenoir City, Tennessee, the first daughter after 5 sons. After mom's birth, there was another son, and another daughter. Ten people in a two-bedroom house, later adding a third bedroom, with no electricity until around 1941, and no indoor plumbing until 1950. My grandfather worked for the city of Lenoir City, and was an electrician, so they were the only household to have electricity, which was a light bulb hanging from a cord. On Saturday nights, her father would put the radio on the front porch, and they would have anywhere from 25-30 people sitting around the yard and on the porch. It was the gathering place to listen to the Grand Ole Opry, Joe Lewis fights, and the news. If the neighbors knew a story was going to be on the radio, they seemed to know my grandfather would not mind taking the radio to the front porch for the neighbors to listen.

Monday was wash day, and she had to be home by 4:30 to help her mother with the chores that were not completed. Twenty shirts and twenty pairs of overalls were ironed every Monday. My grandmother cooked three meals a day, every day for ten people, and any neighbors that stopped by for a visit. They must have eaten a large amount of pinto beans, because I cannot recall one time that my mother cooked and served us pinto beans. On weekends many house cleaning jobs took place along with meal preparation. As you can imagine, gender roles were very defined at that time in society. She recounted to my brother, Mark, while she was cleaning, her brothers were playing football for their school. They didn't share much in the work except for splitting wood, carrying in coal, and mowing the yard. She did acknowledge that football was exhausting, and they didn't have a car, so walking was their mode of transportation, and with lots of homework, by the end of the day, everyone was exhausted.

School was very important to my mother, and she loved her time in the classroom, and with her friends. She was president of her junior class, took piano lessons, sang in the chorus, and played basketball as a guard, because her friends thought she would be tough coming from a household with 6 boys. She graduated from high school in 1949, and really wanted to go to college, but her father did not want her to attend, thinking that women should stay at home and work. He only had an 8th grade education. She was very determined to attend college but knew she would have to apply for grants and scholarships. She asked her English teacher, whose husband was the superintendent of schools, and she received a scholarship to the old Andrew Jackson Business College in Nashville, Tennessee. She would live with a family and care for their children in exchange for room and board. She attended summer school at the

University of Tennessee, and then left in August for Nashville to care for the children of a law professor at Vanderbilt. She attended classes during the day, took care of the children from 4:00 pm until bedtime and then began homework. After a year she received a diploma in business education, moved back to Lenoir City, and became the secretary of First Baptist Church, Lenoir City, at a salary of $28 per week.

About a year later, she left the job at the church, and was hired for various positions at Oak Ridge Nuclear Lab, in Oak Ridge, TN. At first, she worked with the secretarial pool at Y-12 and X-10, but then received a permanent assignment in the medical office conducting multiphasic screening with a salary of $70 per week, more money than she could ever have imagined. She saved some of her money but sent back some of it to help her family, especially her only sister, 7 years her junior. She described her sister's position in the family as being low on the totem pole.

My parents were married August 22, 1952, they moved to Fort Worth, Texas, and my grandfather died three months later. My mother was the apple of my grandfather's eye. After all the boys were born, he was happy to have a girl. He was happy that his daughter was getting married, but would not walk her down the aisle, and didn't want her moving so far away. Momma has said more than once, "If a marriage should not have made it, ours would be a test, because I had such a hard time that first year." She married at 20, and her father died when she was 21. Indeed a very hard first year.

I always remember Momma being home, taking on the traditional role of homemaker, but when I entered the first grade, she worked at the middle school library, but I don't recall the length of time. After I left for college, she attended and graduated from business college and worked in the College of Education, emphasis on adult education, at The University of Tennessee. She was in her element. After understanding the deep desire for her personal education, it seems she was just the right person to encourage adult students; they loved her, and she loved her job. She retired in 1993, just in time to enjoy her grandchildren.

Our house was filled with antique furniture that Momma found, stripped multiple layers of paint, sanded and finished, then proudly displayed them in our house. She could sniff out an ugly piece of furniture and unveil beauty. She also knew quality as well. My brother has our Lazy Susan dining room table that we sat around since I was 2 years old. I have our pedestal kitchen table, the only table I remember in our kitchen.

One of Momma's greatest gifts was hospitality. She always welcomed guests into her house with great fanfare. There was always something delicious to eat, lots of stories to tell, and genuine conversation. I have had numerous people tell me the comfortable atmosphere my mother and father presented in their home. When I took college friends home they always asked when they would be able to return. One of the most endearing characteristics of my Momma and Daddy's hospitality was when guests would leave. They would escort the guests to the door, stand on the porch and wave until the guests were out of sight. I so appreciate this gesture, as it felt like they were offering a covering of protection.

Momma loved her family deeply and was devoted to my grandmother. After my grandfather's death, Momma was always taking care of my grandmother, even if she lived out of state. When we moved to Crossville, Tennessee she visited regularly, as it was only about 1.5 hours away. Momma was in charge of the family reunion to keep the extended family connected. Her brothers and sister talked regularly, and visited often, and looked to her as the matriarch of the family. When my uncles began to pass away I could see the toll it took on Momma. She saw her connections to family disappear, and feared she would be the only one left, and indeed, she was the last sibling to die.

When my brothers and I were going through papers and items in my parent's home I saw so many connections to family. Many pictures of her siblings, family reunions, her parents, letters, and stacks and stacks of papers. Her family was everything to her, and she made great effort to keep them connected by reaching out in various ways, including hours of genealogy research at various libraries in East Tennessee.

Grandchildren were her greatest pleasure, and she was proud of each of them. But she was especially proud of her granddaughters, because she knew it was going to be more challenging for them to achieve the same as her grandsons. Lisa, whose career has moved her to higher levels, and is an advocate for the marginalized in the community, and boldly speaks the truth; Susanna, who has a career, and is a mother; Lydia, who is a medical doctor, and Gabriella who is in the top of her class in law school. I wish she could see them now. Her heart would be bursting with pride.

Mothers are complicated people, and the relationship with their siblings and children are filled with love, conflict and joy. A great Southern writer, Lewis Grizzard, wrote multiple books based on Southern humor and culture. The one that is foremost in my mind right now is, *Don't Forget To Call Your Mama... I Wish I Could Call Mine.*

When I Am Among The Trees

When I am among the trees,
especially the willows and the honey locust,
equally the beech, the oaks and the pines,
they give off such hints of gladness.
I would almost say that they save me, and daily.

I am so distant from the hope of myself,
in which I have goodness, and discernment,
and never hurry through the world
but walk slowly and bow often.
Around me the trees stir in their leaves
and call out, "Stay awhile."
The light flows from their branches.

And they call again, "It's simple," they say,
"and you too have come
into the world to do this, to go easy, to be filled
with light, and to shine."

-Mary Oliver, American poet, Pulitzer prize for poetry, (1935-2019)

We need Joy as we need air. We need Love as we need water. We need each other as we need the earth we share.

-Maya Angelou, American memoirist, poet, civil rights activist (1928-2014)

410 West 40th Street

Located in Hell's Kitchen in New York City is a small community of progressive Baptists who are like none I have ever met. My initial contact with Metro Baptist was after my first semester of seminary. I wanted to engage in urban ministry and had heard this church would welcome volunteers for several weeks at a time. Rev. Tiffany Triplett-Henkel was my initial contact and agreed to allow me a two-week internship to assist with the after kids program, ESOL, food distribution, and preparation for Summer Clue Camp. The two weeks were very impactful, as I had never been in a church with so much cultural diversity. It was refreshing to worship with people who spoke multiple languages, who had skin very different from mine, and who were open members of the LGBTQ community. Metro doesn't hide who they are. They display the following words: "Metro Baptist Church is a Christian community where all are welcome regardless of gender, age, sexual identity, ethnicity, social standing, education, or economic standing. We believe that everyone is created by God in the likeness of God to be a full participant in God's redemptive plan."

After two weeks with Metro, I wondered if there would be additional opportunities to participate with the congregation. The following summer I found myself in New York City for three months as a hospital chaplain resident at Memorial Sloan Kettering Cancer Center, and during my time in The Big Apple, I attended Metro. I began to involve myself with the events of the congregation and realized this was home. As a seminary student who was pursuing hospital chaplaincy, I knew ordination would be in my future and that Metro would be the church I would request for ordination. That involved becoming a member of Metro Baptist Church and participating from a distance as I was living in Tennessee. My ordination process took place three years later, and on August 5, 2012, the beautiful congregation of Metro Baptist Church ordained me to the gospel ministry and blessed me with their support and love.

Rev. Tiffany Triplett-Henkel, Rev. Alan Sherouse, Rev. David Fleenor, Rev. Mary Beth Duke, and Dr. Molly Marshall participated in my ordination service, along with my children and my mother. It was an emotionally impactful day that affirmed my decision to follow in my father's footsteps of ministry and support for pursuing hospital chaplaincy. The day also proclaimed me as a woman in ministry, a place that has not always been welcoming. Because of Metro's bold stance for inclusion, ordaining a woman was not looked upon as unique or unusual, but a natural decision of the church community.

Even though I am not physically present with the congregation of Metro Baptist Church, I continue to hold them tightly and pray for their continued impact at 410 West 40th St.

Mountain Memories

O ye Mountains, robed in grandeur,
    Ye have dazed mine eyes with light,
'Till all other things lack beauty,~
    Seeming paltry to your might.

Ye have borne me to your summits
    Where the air is heavenly pure.
Now the breath in valleys lurking
    Is oppressive to endure.

Ye have opened boundless wonders
    Where my fearless eyes could rove.
Now I pine for wide horizons
    In the limits of a grove.

But the bondage is less galling
    Than unfettered liberty
With no wish, no innate power
    To declare my spirit free.

-**Ruby Archer**, *American poet (1873-1961)*

Native American Prayer

Oh, Great Spirit
Whose voice I hear in the winds,
And whose breath gives life to all the world,
hear me. I am small and weak,
I need your strength and wisdom.
Let me walk in beauty and make my eyes ever behold
the red and purple sunset.
Make my hands respect the things you have
made and my ears sharp to hear your voice.
Make me wise so that I may understand the things
you have taught my people
Let me learn the lessons you have
hidden in every leaf and rock.

I seek strength, not to be greater than my brother,
but to fight my greatest enemy - myself.
Make me always ready to come to you
with clean hands and straight eyes.
So when life fades, as the fading sunset,
my Spirit may come to you without shame.

(translated by Lakota Sioux Chief Yellow Lark in 1887) published in Native American Prayers - by the Episcopal Church

Gracious God, your amazing love extends through all time and space, to all parts of your creation, which you created and called good. You made a covenant with Noah and his family, putting a rainbow in the sky to symbolize your promise of love and blessing to every living creature, and to all successive generations. You made a covenant with Abraham and Sarah, blessing them and their descendants throughout the generations. You made a covenant with Moses and the Israelite people to all generations, giving them the 10 commandments and challenging them to choose life. In Jesus, you invite us to enter into a new covenant, in communion with all who seek to be faithful to you. As people of faith, we are called into covenant. Your covenant of faithfulness and love extends to the whole creation. We pray for the healing of the earth, that present and future generations may enjoy the fruits of creation, and continue to glorify and praise you.

-National Council of Churches

Nature Aria

Autumn mind chases in
From all directions
And a thousand chaste leaves
Give way.

Scatter in me the seeds
Of a thousand saplings.
Let grow a grassy heaven.
On my brow: a sun.
This bliss is yours, Living
World, and alone it endures.
Music at midnight.
Young wine.
Lovers hand in hand
By daylight, moonlight.
Living World, hold me
In your mouth,

Slip on your frivolous shoes
And dance with me. My soul
Is the wild vine
Who alone has grasped it,
Who has seen through the awful plot,
Who will arrive in time to vanquish
The river already heavy with blossoms,
The moon spilling light onto packs

Of men. What is sadder than witless
Wolves, wind without borders,
Nationless birds, small gifts
Laden with love's intentions?

Fistfuls of rain fall hard, fill
My heart with mud. An old wind
May still come chasing in.
Resurrection fire. And me here
Laughing like a cloud in trousers,
Entreating the earth to bury me.

-**Yi Lei,** Chinese Poet (1951-2018) translated by Tracy K. Smith and Changtai Bi

In the summer of 1877, a group of about 800 Nez Perce (NiMiiPuu) men, women, and children, and nearly 2000 horses, fled their homeland of the Wallowa Mountains in Oregon/Idaho to seek refuge from forced relocation by the U.S. Army. They fled from the Army eastward 1,170 miles over the span of four months, spending 13 days in what was, at the time, a newly established Yellowstone National Park. Ultimately, hundreds of U.S. soldiers and Nez Perce (including women and children) were killed along their flight before the Nez Perce surrendered. Some of the Nez Perce were able to reach Canada, but the rest accepted resettlement in numerous reservations throughout the country.

As part of the 150 anniversary of Yellowstone National Park, members of the Nez Perce Appaloosa Horse Club and Yellowstone staff ride sections of the Nez Perce Trail in the park to connect Nez Perce youth and adults to the trail, their history, and ancestors. Following the ride, members coordinated a horse parade in traditional regalia, danced, and told stories about the history and culture of the NiMiiPuu.

-Yellowstone National Park Facebook Page

By the beginning of the 20th century, the Nez Perce had declined to about 1,800. The tribe reports having more than 3,500 members in 2021.

O' GREAT SPIRIT
help me always
to speak the truth quietly,
to listen with an open mind
when others speak,
and to remember the peace
that may be found in silence.

Cherokee Prayer

Leave the roads; take the trails.

-**Pythagoras**, ancient Ionian Greek philosopher (c.570-c.495 BC)

Light and Darkness, night and day.
We marvel at the mystery of the stars.
Moon and sky, sand and sea.
We marvel at the mystery of the sun.
Twilight, high noon, dusk and dawn.
Though we are mortal, we are Creation's crown.
Flesh and bone, steel and stone.
We dwell in fragile, temporary shelters.
Grant steadfast love, compassion, grace.
Sustain us, Lord; our origin is dust.
Splendor, mercy, majesty, love endure.
We are but little lower than the angels.
Resplendent skies, sunset, sunrise.
The grandeur of Creation lifts our lives.
Evening darkness, morning dawn.
Renew our lives as You renew all time.

-The Rabbinical Assembly of the United Synagogue of America

Praised are you Adonai our God,
who rules the universe,
which lack nothing;
for God created fine creatures
and pleasant trees in order that
humans might enjoy them.

-The Rabbinical Assembly of Conservative Judaism

There is something infinitely healing in the repeated refrains of nature - the assurance that dawn comes after night, and spring after winter.

-Rachel Carson, American marine biologist, writer and conservationist (1907-1964)

Adopt the pace of nature: her secret is patience.

-**Ralph Waldo Emerson**, American essayist, lecturer, philosopher, abolitionist, poet (1803-1882)

Rita Ayers Crowder
December 27, 1960 - January 2, 2021

The snow angel in this picture is in memory of Rita Ayers Crowder. Our paths never had direct contact, but we crossed through her beloved sister and my dear friend, Anita Ayers Henderlight.

Anita has been described as a sparkler, spreading light and leaving her shine in the wake of darkness. But if Anita is a sparkler, evidently Rita was a full-blown fireworks spectacular complete with choreographed music.

In early November 2020, Rita was admitted to the hospital with symptoms of Covid-19. That was when Anita introduced Rita to the world. Stories and pictures were posted on social media as many of us were introduced to the life that was Rita Crowder. Prayers, loving thoughts, and support of her family were shared as Covid-19 took Rita's life on January 2, 2021. The outpouring of love for Rita and her family was a beautiful demonstration of love. Anita asked for birthday cards as Rita's birthday was December 27. Cards flooded her ICU room, and the dedicated nursing staff hung the birthday wishes around her room.

Why a snow angel? A video surfaced online of Rita, impeccably dressed, leaving work after a snowfall. Perhaps on a dare, or maybe she couldn't help herself,

Rita lay down in the parking lot and made a snow angel. The laughter on the video was contagious. The snow angel became a symbol of support for Rita. Anita's Facebook page was flooded with friends making angels in the snow, sand, dirt, and grass. Some were drawn with pens, markers, pencils, even lipstick.

The following was said about Rita on her funeral home's condolences page:

"Rita was a shining example of how to live a life of service to others. She was a passionate advocate for her team, her residents, and her family. She was constantly doing random acts of kindness like being the first one to wish you a happy birthday or giving you a pick me up compliment which would make you smile, but they also meant a lot coming from her as she was always impeccably dressed and put together. Most of all, I will miss how she started every interaction with a smile and ended most with a hug. She will be missed by all who knew her."

Be like Rita!!!

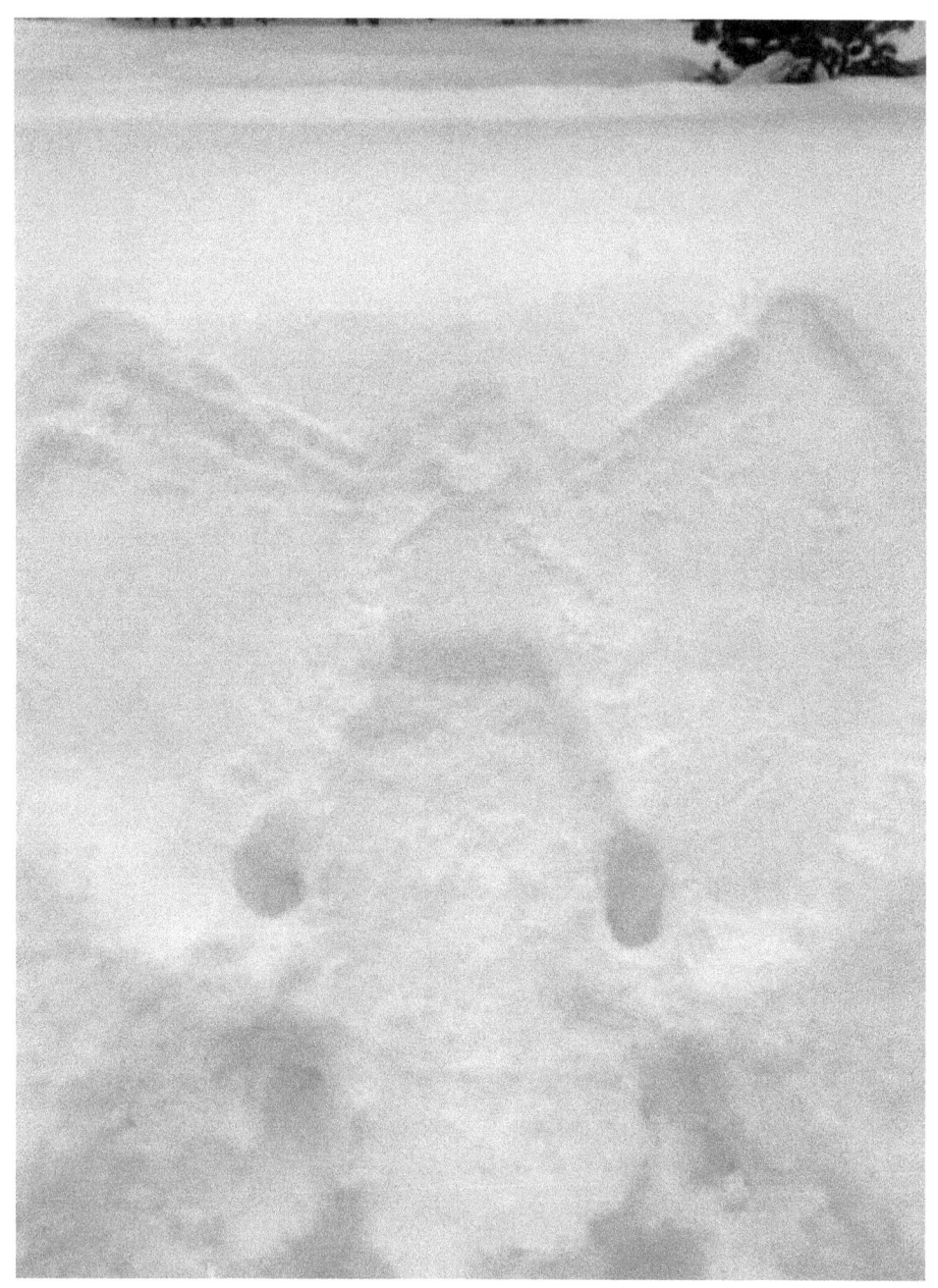

Knowing that you love the earth changes you, activates you to defend and protect and celebrate. But when you feel that the earth loves you in return, that feeling transforms the relationship from a one-way street into a sacred bond.

-Robin Wall Kimmerer, *Braiding Sweetgrass: Indigenous Wisdom, Scientific Knowledge and the Teachings of Plants* American Distinguished Teaching Professor of Environmental and Forest Biology, b. 1953

Significant Marks

Luke 24:13-35

With today's scripture passage, I am moving you back. Moving you back to a time immediately after Easter. A time when we celebrate the resurrection of Christ. A time when the churches are so packed there is standing room only. I am taking you back to a time when Jesus revealed himself to his disciples.

He was walking down the road to Emmaus, a little village about seven miles from Jerusalem.

He joined with two of his followers, and as they talked and were conversing they had not a clue he was the risen Christ walking among them. They were talking about the events of the crucifixion, the burial and resurrection, but Jesus did not let on that he was the very person that they were talking about. Now this was very fresh information in their minds, and he began to ask them details, perhaps wanting to get their version of the story. They even asked him, "Are you the only stranger in this town? Do you not know what has been happening the past few days? Because if you had been here you would not have asked us about the story we are discussing." Throughout the entire discussion and the latest breaking information, Jesus remained incognito. That is until they persuaded him to stay and dine with them. They joined with the other disciples in the Upper Room, and as they were sharing a meal and conversing around the table, Jesus took the bread, blessed, broke it and gave it to them. At that very moment, the disciples' eyes were opened, and they recognized him, but not for long, because he vanished from their sight.

Their astonishment must have been completely unbelievable because their idea of a bodily resurrection was not clear. Not all believed in the actual physical bodily resurrection. Some thought he died, but now he was alive, but only as a spirit. Others believed Jesus only appeared to have died on the cross, because as the Son of God, he only appeared to be of human flesh. While the disciples were talking about this and discussing whether it was really Jesus or was it an apparition, he came back. He stood among them and said, "Shalom, peace be with you." Judging from their responses, Jesus seemed to know the disciples still failed to understand that he was alive. He was not a resuscitated corpse, nor a ghost, or a spirit, but a resurrected life, real flesh and bones standing before them. He began to speak with them, and as he attempted to help them understand he really was Jesus, he didn't say "I am Jesus, listen to my voice." He also didn't say "Look at my face, oh don't you remember my face?" No, he asked them to notice his hands and his feet.

I doubt anyone here, unless you are a hand and foot model, is noticed by your hands and feet. We aren't recognized by them. There are people who have very talented hands who can take a piece of wood and craft it into a beautiful piece of furniture, or who play an instrument and use their hands to produce glorious music. My sister-in-law is an interpreter for the deaf, and her hands are beautiful as she signs for the deaf and hearing impaired. If I were to ask you to pull out pictures of your significant other or your children or your grandchildren, would it be a picture of a face or a picture of hands? What about our feet? They are much more private than our hands and really aren't as pretty. We cover them and sometimes abuse them with fashionable shoes that pinch our toes. New York City feet must be particularly abused because I can't get on a bus or the subway without seeing an ad for a podiatrist. We may try to dress them up with a pedicure, but they continue to be members of our body that are not on display. They bear the calluses of walking, standing, and running.

Barbara Brown Taylor, author, priest, and professor, indicates it was the wounds that Jesus wanted the disciples to notice. They had seen him nailed on the cross. They watched as Jesus was stretched out, and the spikes driven into his hands. They heard the cries of agony as the hammer hit the head of the spikes. Jesus was the only person walking around Jerusalem with nail holes in his hands and feet. And I wonder were those markings the only thing to have made the disciples believe in Jesus' resurrection? If Jesus had asked them to look at his face or listen to his voice, that would not have been absolute proof. But his wounds were unmistakable. All of Jerusalem was there to witness his crucifixion; they knew he had wounds.

But before Jesus presented the wounds of his hands and feet as proof of his resurrection, the disciples had witnessed his hands and feet in so many other capacities. His were the hands that blessed the five loaves and two fishes as he fed the 5000. They were the same hands that made a muddy paste and placed it on the eyes of a blind man. They brought to life Jairus' young daughter. They touched the marginalized members of the community, including lepers, the crippled and demonic. His feet took him through the countryside to the home of Simon, where a questionable woman wept at his feet and dried them with her hair. Another woman, whose reputation was also in question, poured expensive perfume on his feet. A woman who had been bleeding for 12 years touched his clothing but fell at his feet. His dirty, calloused, smelly feet.

It would have been so much easier for Jesus to have returned all crisp and clean and whole. That might have taken away some of the guilt for those who fled and denied they even knew him. Perhaps some of the disciples' astonishment at Jesus' appearance was because they were afraid of retaliation. Instead, Jesus showed them the danger was past. He wanted them to know he had gone through the danger and not around it. His hands and feet told them the truth of what had happened to him, which was the only proof he had that he was who he said he was.

Several years ago there was a book that hit the shelves; it was a somewhat controversial book, and, of course, it became one of my favorites. *The Shack* by William P. Young tells the story of Mackenzie Allen Phillips and his encounter with God. McKenzie's young daughter had been murdered, and the continued grief he experienced was referred to as the Great Sadness. As Mackenzie attempted to deal with his Great Sadness, he returned to the shack where his daughter was murdered, all at the invitation of God, who is called Papa. Much to Mackenzie's surprise, Papa is a large African American woman who is exuberant, an excellent cook, and one who gives hugs that squeeze the very stuffing out of you. Early in the encounter, while Papa is preparing the pie crust for the evening's dessert, Mackenzie notices there are scars on Papa's wrists. He studied the scars, stared, and tried to not be obvious. Papa saw Mackenzie stare; she allowed him to touch the scars, outlining the deep piercing, feeling the skin, the skin once smooth and soft, but now rough and uneven. With tears streaming down her flour-dusted cheeks, Papa responded, " Mackenzie, don't ever think what my son chose to do didn't cost us dearly. Love always leaves a significant mark." Think of all the love that had been shone through Jesus' hands and feet. Ponder the love Jesus showed to his disciples, that their friend, confidant and teacher, died a cruel death. Alone. Dejected and rejected; they did not deserve grace, but they received it anyway.

Tennessee-born recording artist Michael Card wrote and performed a song entitled "Why?" In that song, he asked many questions, including: "Why did it have to be a friend who betrayed the Lord?" "Why did he use a kiss, because that is not what a kiss is for?" "Why did it have to be a heavy cross he was made to bear, and why did they nail his hands and feet? His love would have held him there." Jesus bore the scars. Everything he did from birth to death to resurrection was for love, and the love he gave left a significant mark.

During my life, I have been marked by very special people who have shaped me, molded me, and prepared me for the events of this day. And several of them are here: my mother, Mary Nickell, Lydia, Phillip and Gabriella, but there is one who is absent, my father. Rev. Joseph Nickell. He suffers from advanced Alzheimer's Disease, but although he is not physically present, his love and support have pierced the deepest parts of my life and have left an incredible and significant mark.

I encourage you to think about your significant mark. Throughout this summer, various groups have traveled long distances to work with the children of Clue Camp, leaving a significant mark. The interns who we honor today have worked with all the special groups of the church and have left a significant mark. This congregation, you who open your doors wide to the community, you produce fruits and vegetables from the rooftop garden, you teach English to speakers of other languages, you provide homework help to school-aged children, you provide a safe haven of activities in the teen center, and so much more. And you leave a significant mark. There is no one here who has not been marked by love because as a child of God there is nothing that can separate us from God's love.

I would like to leave you with a quote from Catholic Archbishop Fulton Sheen: "When Christ comes for us he will look for the marks of the cross on each of us. He will look to see what sacrifices we have made. Will our hands be scratched and sore from looking for lost sheep? Will our feet be calloused and bruised from walking tirelessly to share the good news?"

As you walk from this place today and every day following the example of our risen Christ, let your love leave a significant mark.

This sermon was preached on the occasion of my ordination by Metro Baptist Church, New York City, August 5, 2012.

Sonnet

I had no thought of violets of late,
The wild, shy kind that spring beneath your feet
In wistful April days, when lovers mate
And wander through the fields in raptures sweet.
The thought of violets means florists' shops,
And bows and pins, and perfumed papers fine;
And garish lights, and mincing little tops
And cabarets and songs, and deadening wine.
So far from sweet real things my thoughts had strayed,
I had forgot wide fields, and clear brown streams;
The perfect loveliness that God has made,--
Wild violets shy and Heaven-mounting dreams.
And now-unwittingly, you've made me dream
Of violets, and my soul's forgotten gleam.

-Alice Moore Dunbar-Nelson, American poet, journalist, activist (1875-1935)

O God, enlarge within us the sense of
fellowship with all living things,
our brothers the animals to whom thou
gavest the earth as their home in
common with us.
We remember with shame that in the past
we have exercised the high dominion
of man with ruthless cruelty
so that the voice of the earth,
which should have gone up to thee
in song, has been a groan of travail.

May we realize that they live not for
us alone but for themselves and for
thee, and that they love
the sweetness of life.

-**St. Basil the Great,** Bishop of Caesarea (329-379)

Sunset

I saw the day lean o'er the world's sharp edge,
And peer into night's chasm, dark and damp.
High in his hand he held a blazing lamp,
Then dropped it and plunged headlong down the ledge.

With lurid splendor that swift paled to gray,
I saw the dim skies suddenly flush bright.
'Twas but the expiring glory of the light
Flung from the hand of the adventurous day.

-**Ella Wheeler Wilcox**, American poet and author (1850-1919)

-Photograph captured by Lydia Prevost

"I felt my lungs inflate with the onrush of scenery - air, mountains, trees, people. I thought, "This is what it is to be happy.""

-Sylvia Plath, American poet, (1932-1963)

John Claypool

During the mid-1950s, my parents lived in Louisville, Kentucky, where my father was studying at Southern Baptist Theological Seminary. They became friends with John and Lue Ann Claypool.

I don't have many stories from my parents about their friendship with the Claypool's, but I know it was one of fondness and respect.

If you have been associated in Baptist or Episcopal circles, you have heard of John Claypool, have read his books and perhaps heard him preach. The book that was very personal for him, and perhaps his most well-known was *Tracks of A Fellow Struggler*, comprising four sermons that describe his spiritual journey during his daughter's illness and after her death. Laura Lue was diagnosed with leukemia and after an 18-month battle with the disease, she died at age 10. While processing the enormous grief of Laura Lue's death, John viewed life as a gift, not something to be earned or taken as a possession. "...if we are willing, the experience of grief can deepen and widen our ability to participate in life. We can become more grateful for the gifts we have been given, more open handed in our handling of the events of life, more sensitive to the whole mysterious process of life, and more trusting in our adventure with God." (Claypool)

Fast forward to 2002 when John was diagnosed with advanced multiple myeloma. It was during this time that I was training and coaching with the Leukemia/Lymphoma Team in Training, raising money for the organization. Cyclists from all over the United States, including our group from Knoxville, Tennessee, rode our bicycles around Lake Tahoe as part of the fundraising efforts.

I contacted John, using my parents name for familiarization, introduced myself and asked if I could raise money in his honor. He returned a beautifully handwritten note with deep appreciation and enthusiasm. Over the course of several months we exchanged notes, which I keep in my important papers file. He was always gracious, kind and authentic. When I received the email on September 3, 2005, telling me that John had died, I sat at my computer and cried. This kind and gentle man, who was a giant in the world of theology, was humbled that his name would be pinned to my cycling jersey.

At John's memorial service in Louisville, Kentucky at Crescent Hill Baptist Church, John's son, Rowan, shared a story about riding in a taxicab in Hong Kong, and when the name Claypool was mentioned, the driver turned to Rowan and asked if they were talking about John Claypool. I found this to be true in Lake Tahoe. Several people saw John's name on my jersey and commented on his books, or they had heard him preach.

I am very grateful to have experienced a small segment of John's enormous and influential life, and will forever remember his words, "Life is a gift."

The happiest people I've ever met, regardless of their profession, their social standing, or their economic status, are people that are fully engaged in the world around them. The most fulfilled people are the ones who get up every morning and stand for something larger than themselves. They are the people who care about others, who will extend a helping hand to someone in need or will speak up about an injustice when they see it.

-Wilma Mankiller, Native American activist, social worker, community developer and the first woman elected to serve as Principal Chief of the Cherokee Nation (1945-2010)

Wedding Officiant

June 26, 2015 was one of the greatest days in our nation's history, as the United States Supreme Court struck down all state's bans on same-sex marriage, legalized it in all fifty states, and required states to honor out-of-state same-sex marriage licenses. The rainbow in the sky took on new symbolism that day as anyone who loved someone else could be married, and it was legal!

As a resident of East Tennessee, I lived in the Bible Belt. Not only in the Bible Belt, but in the middle of the cross on the buckle of the Bible Belt. I also lived next door to the county that is second to Las Vegas in the number of marriage certificates issued. Yes, Sevier County, with Dollywood, Pigeon Forge, Gatlinburg, Sevierville and the Great Smoky Mountains, is second to Las Vegas. I knew there would be same-sex couples who wanted to be married and would not be able to find an open and affirming officiant, so I decided to join the wedding officiant industry. A website was set up, pictures were taken, and a biographical profile was included. The outcome was unbelievable, as same-sex and opposite-sex couples wanted to be married in Sevier County. The couples I met were from all over the United States, some traveling with families, some with only the closest of friends, and a few were elopements. They were delightful, gracious, and so happy to be wed in one of the most beautiful areas of our state. Facebook has continued to keep some of us connected and watching the changes in their lives has been very gratifying.

Love for another is an emotional bond that joins us together. It weaves together our differences into a fabric that represents who we are together. Making the pronouncement, "It is my great honor and privilege to present to you for the first time as a married couple," has been one of the greatest honors of my life.

Acknowledgements

It is my hope that you enjoyed this book of stories, poems, prayers, quotes and pictures, taken by my iPhone 11. A huge thank you to David Tullock and Parsons Porch for publishing this collection.

Bridget Lewellen, whose wedding I officiated in the Great Smoky Mountains, English teacher for 23 years, read the stories, and provided excellent edits.

There are many friends who have encouraged and supported me along the journey, and I would not be here without them. Holly Kelly, who offers me a homebase; Elizabeth Nipper, who is always supportive, and offers great encouragement; Anita Henderlight, who always checks on my whereabouts; Tammy Petty Brewer, who knows I am well when we exchange our daily Wordle; and my family, who does not think I have completely lost my mind and may have benefited from my travels.

Shalom!

www.ingramcontent.com/pod-product-compliance
Lightning Source LLC
Chambersburg PA
CBHW051545010526
44118CB00022B/2586